Thank You
for My Grandchild

Thank You for My Grand-child

BETTY ISLER

Concordia
Publishing House
St. Louis

Copyright© 1983 Corcordia Publishing House
3558 S. Jefferson Avenue, St. Louis, MO 63118
Manufactured in the United States of America

Library of Congress Cataloging in Publication Data

Isler, Betty, 1915 —
    Thank you for my grandchild.

    1. Grandmothers — Prayer-books and devotions — English
I. Title.
BV4847.I83   1983   242'.85   83-7569
ISBN 0-570-03915-0 (pbk.)

1 2 3 4 5 6 7 8 9 10   PP   92 91 90 89 88 87 86 85 84 83

This book is for Sally, Sharon, and Jamie.

Contents

We Have Become Grandparents! 11
Each New Child 13
This Child Is Yours 14
My New Role 15
Bedtime 16
Viewpoint 17
Laughing Boy 18
Father's Day 19
The Loving Reach 20
Diamonds and Rubies 21
"Suffer the Little Children" 22
In the Kitchen 23
The Dove 24
The Coloring Book 25
Love Can Be a Chocolate Chip Cookie 26
Things Seen and Unseen 27
Happy Birthday to Nanny 28
The Gift 29
His Upside-Down World 30
Stormy Weather 31
Surprise Visit 32
The Recital 33
Overnight Guest 34
Young Artist 35
After a Day in the Park 36

There Are Days 37
The Speedster 38
"God Rest Ye Merry, Gentlemen" 39
The Open Arms 40
Departure 41
The Mailman Comes at 10:00 42
While We Are Apart 43
The Visit 44
The Homecoming 45
Thanksgiving Grace 46
Obedience 47
Sibling Love 48
"I Will Not Leave You Comfortless. . . ." 49
Rescue Mission 50
My Line of No Resistance 51
The Miniature 52
Eternal Season 53
Precious Possession 54
Team Effort 55
No Room in the Inn 56
The Dinner Party 57
"I Bring You Good Tidings" 58
A Growing Boy 59
The Steward 60
The New Roller Skates 61
I Have My Limits 62
Picture Lighting 63
Running the Course 64
Alfred, the Duck 65

My Contract Has Not Been Renewed 66
Delayed Input 67
No Longer the Little One 68
Credibility Gap 69
Confirmation 70
The Mechanic 71
The Collision 72
No Greater Love 73
Looking Ahead 74
Mother and Daughter Banquet 75
Winds of Tomorrow 76
Growth Pattern 77
Junior Prom 78
The Graduate 79
Quietly Now 80

We Have Become Grandparents!

I had thought that surely heavenly trumpets would sound when we hurried to the hospital to see this first, long-awaited grandchild. I expected angelic choirs to burst into thunderous anthems, for church bells to ring, for voices to be raised in triumphant acclaim. There was nothing. Just a business-as-usual, ordinary day along the colorless corridors of the maternity floor of Westminster Community Hospital.

We stood outside the glass-enclosed nursery with a scattering of other people whom we did not know, and stared at the cluster of small, identical cribs, holding small, identical blanket-wrapped newborns. We held up the visitor's card to the glass for the nurse inside to read, and waited while she turned without hestiation to *that* particular crib, and picked up *that* particular baby and brought him to the window for us to see. She opened the blanket and showed us our grandson, peacefully sleeping, and in that instant my good spouse and I were transported into another world of delight and wonder, all our own. Never mind the trumpets and church bells. Here in this sweet continuation of life we saw Your miracle, performed quietly again, just for us!

Of course, that is how You planned it, isn't it, Lord? That no birth of a child can ever be ordinary, that each infant, in itself, is another small private miracle.

It has been the same for us with the birth of each succeeding grandchild. The bright expectancy does not tarnish, the wonder does not diminish. Each child is unique and special to us, and equally cherished.

Oh! Thank You, Lord, for grandchildren!

Each New Child

Lord,
How do You do it?

You create each child
To a different pattern,
As varied as the glass fragments
In a kaleidoscope
That fall with the merest
Whisper of movement
Into unique designs,
Each tiny piece
Slipping into place
To make another
Exquisite new whole,
Never to be
Duplicated.

Each time a child is born,
The pieces shift and change,
Settling into one more
Distinct combination,
Delicately coordinated,
Another intricate unit,
Made more beautiful
By Your light
Shining through it.

Lord,
How do You do it?

This Child is Yours

Seven pounds, six ounces,
Blue eyes, a wisp of hair,
Incredibly small fingers
Softly curled,
Only ten days into the world,
So unaware.

Tenderly borne to the altar,
More precious than gold,
This new little lamb
Is brought to Your fold.

My New Role

They don't do things now
The way I did
When his mother
Was an infant,
So I must learn how
All over again!

It's a whole new approach,
And Lord,
I'm willing to try it
If You will help me
To keep quiet.

Bedtime

I sing the same lullabies
I sang to his mother,
And watch the dark lashes
Drop slowly onto
The small, soft cheek,
Holding that warm stillness
In my arms
As I rock him
To sleep.

Lord,
These are the memories
Women keep.

Viewpoint

Lord,
As a parent I felt—
No ifs, buts, or maybes—
Of all Your creations,
The greatest
Are babies.

I can now report,
With unabashed candor,
GRANDbabies
Are grander!

Laughing Boy

He is such a sunny child.
Mirth bubbles up from him
In a fountain of
Chuckles and
Giggles and
Grins.

He finds life
A high comedy
In which he has a
Starring part,
And his laughter
Is tonic for the heart.

Thank You, Lord,
For this small package
Of enormous joy!

18

Father's Day

They stand together
On the front lawn
For their picture,
Great-grandfather,
Grandfather,
Father and
Son.

Pride and pleasure
Caught by the camera,
From the gentle smile
On great grandpop
Right down to the grin
On the littlest one.

Oh! Thank You, Lord,
For these generations,
Young and old,
Blessings
Four-fold!

19

The Loving Reach

He has a new baby sister
And is worried that
I will not be able
To hold both of them
In the rocking chair.

I tell him that
God gives grandmothers
Extra-long arms
That can reach around
All their children
With inches to spare.

And of course it's true.
You really do, Lord.
You really do!

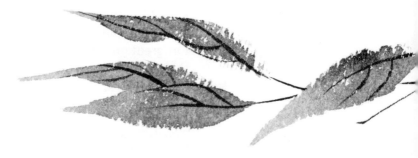

Diamonds and Rubies

Lord,
I am not one
To place high value
On material gifts
Or things of this earth.

But today my grandson
Has bestowed upon me
Jewels of inestimable
Worth.

From his Easter basket
He has lovingly extracted
All the black jelly beans for me
Because he knows
I like them best.

Lord, I am truly
Licorice blessed!

"Suffer the Little Children"

Jesus, tender Shepherd,
Extend Your limitless patience
To this shy little lamb,
Our three-year-old granddaughter,
Who sits through her entire
Prekindergarten
Sunday school class
With her blanket
Over her head!

Let her learn, instead,
To exchange this shelter
For the safe, warm haven
Of Your love.

In the Kitchen

She is "helping" me
With the dishes today,
Standing on a chair
To reach the sink.

My apron drags
Soddenly around her feet
As she shows me
How she can make soap bubbles
By blowing through
Her little clenched fist.

She watches the iridescent globes
Float across the counter
Until they burst
On contact.

Lord,
I pray she will always bring
Such sparkle to homey chores,
Knowing an inner satisfaction
That does not vanish
The instant it meets
An obstacle.

The Dove

At the children's zoo
We cannot pry him away
From the walk-through bird cage.
A white dove
Has landed on his shoulder,
Nestling against him
Like a close buddy,
And he is reluctant
To give it release.

Lord,
If I am not reaching too far
For a parallel,
May he always remain close
To Your dove
Of peace.

The Coloring Book

The hall closet
Contains their box of toys.
Like a homing pigeon,
She heads for it
First thing.

Today she decides to color,
Kneeling on the floor,
Scowling with the effort
To stay within the lines.
She is learning
That a disciplined crayon
Produces a better picture.

Lord,
May she always find pleasure
In following Your paths,
Discovering that
Her life can be
A rainbow of beautiful colors
By faithfully tracing
Your footsteps.

Love Can Be
a Chocolate Chip Cookie

In my more
Realistic moments,
Sometimes I feel
That the usefulness
Of grandmothers
Depends a great deal
Upon being skilled
At keeping cookie jars
Filled.

Things Seen and Unseen

Lord,
How can a small boy
Be expected to know
That the rewards
For diligently brushing his teeth
Will show up
In time . . .

When his sister
With the cavities
Comes away from the dentist
With three balloons
And a shiny dime?

Lord,
Help him to learn
That matters of real worth
Are seldom
Of this earth.

Happy Birthday to NANCY

I love greeting cards
With their beautiful art work
And creative design,
Especially those cards
Painstakingly made for me
By these grandchildren of mine:

The lopsided flowers,
The eternally bursting sun,
The assortment of stiff-legged
Cats, dogs, birds, people
And miscellaneous other
Unidentified objects.
I cherish each one.

Could any message of love,
Any museum masterpiece,
Possibly be better
Than such a creation,
Laboriously signed
With a backward letter?

28

The Gift

She is a dreamy child,
And her images of fantasy
Delight me.

On a summer evening
We lie back in the lawn chairs
And watch the stars blink on
In the darkening sky.

She says she wishes she could
Gather a handful of stars
And moonbeams, too.

"What would you do with them?"
I ask, and her reply:
"I would put them in fruit jars
And give them to you!"

His Upside-Down World

I simply do not know
How his parents
Keep him in shoes,
Or how he can
Shred them to tatters
So quickly,
When he spends so much
Of his time
Hanging by his knees
On the jungle gym,
Perilously busy.

It occurs to me
His guardian angel
Must get
Awfully dizzy.

Stormy Weather

Today her face
Is tear-streaked
And her mouth turns down
In unhappiness.

She has been scolded,
And her little world
Is gray and sunless.

She brings me the picture
She has crayoned,
Heavy with dark colors,
Angry, black clouds,
A deep purple house,
Leafless brown trees
With branches drooping
In despair.

She climbs into my lap
And finds comfort with me
In the rocking chair.

Lord, as she grows
Help her to turn
For healing solace
To Your waiting arms
And tender care.

Surprise Visit

They drop in unexpectedly,
Spilling through the front door
Like a rambunctious, impish brook

Overflowing its banks
    In bursting exuberance,
        Bubbling, gurgling,
Spreading out in little rivulets
    Into every corner
        Of the house,
Pushing out the stale air,
    Chattering, chortling,
        Laughing, exploring,
In constant motion and play,
        Bringing a fresh
            And quickening momentum

Into what had been
A dull day.

The Recital

She rattles off
What seem like
A dozen verses of
"Jesus Loves Me,"
Having lost me
After the second.

She continues on,
Her clear little voice
Trilling confidently
Through every other song
She has learned in
Vacation Bible school,
Never hesitating
Over the words
So firmly imbedded
In her eager memory.

She is happy and secure
Because, she wants us to know,
"The Bible tells me so."

Overnight Guest

It is her turn
To spend the night with us.
She comes dragging
Her own small suitcase,
Bulging with supplies
Guaranteed to meet
Any conceivable
Situation:

Her water pistol,
Three marbles,
A favorite book,
A new game
(At which she will beat me),
And of course,
What's left of
Her security blanket.

I tuck her in,
So achingly dear,
Lower the light
And quietly hear
Her prayer,
To which I add my own:

Lord,
In good time and due,
Help her to turn
That security blanket
Over to You.

Young Artist

He loves to copy
His grandfather's drawings.
Intrigued by that gloriously
Black India ink
And Speed Ball pen,
He produces his own
Heavy-handed cartoons
And proudly signs them.

Sometimes I think
His joy is not so much
In the drawing
As getting to use
The ink!

After a Day in the Park

She wants to know
If there is playground equipment
In heaven.

I tell her I think so.

She wants to know
If children are permitted
To rollerskate in heaven.

I tell her I think so.

She wants to know
If angels can ride their bikes
In heaven.

I tell her it wouldn't surprise me.

She ponders this, then asks,
"But how would I keep
My long white gown
From tangling in the spokes?"

I was very glad
The phone rang
Just then.

There Are Days

Lord,
Do I weary You
With my constant
Songs of praise
For these brilliant,
Remarkable,
Precious,
Lovable
Children?

Then, Lord,
Hear this!
Today they are
Impossible,
Quarrelsome,
Belligerent,
Disobedient,
Totally uninterested
In anything
I've shown them!

Forgive me Lord.
I hope their mother
Picks them up
Before I disown them.

The Speedster

Anything on wheels
Has always fascinated
This boy.
Locomotion has been his need
From the earliest toy
Through go-cart,
Tricycle,
Skate board
And now his precious
Ten-speed.

I have just realized
That in a few years
He will become
Motorized!

Lord,
I come to You prayerfully.
Grant him the maturity
To drive carefully!

"God Rest Ye Merry, Gentlemen"

Today we are baking
Christmas cookies.
She is not so concerned
With rolling out the dough
As with the decorating.

With some misgivings
I give her free reign
And let her begin.

Later, my kitchen
Resembles a disaster area
And the gingerbread men
Are all cross-eyed,
But each sticky grin
Is joyously wide.

The Open Arms

She has begged a ride
On the merry-go-round
And excitedly mounts
The bejewelled horse,
Ticket in a tight grip
In her little hand
As she begins her
Up and down trip
Through fantasy land.

She waves cheerfully
Each time she passes.
But when the ride is over
She is disoriented
And panics tearfully
Until I call to her.

Lord,
In her life ahead,
Should she lose direction,
Call her back to the safety
Of Your waiting arms.

Departure

Lord,
The unthinkable has happened!
This dear, young family
Whom we love the most
Is suddenly being transferred
To the East Coast.

Go with them, Lord.

We wave bravely
As they pull away
From the curb,
Loaded with baggage
And every vestige
Of themselves,
Including the cat!

Go with them, Lord.

How lonely without them,
How empty and still.
Lord, I suspect
We are going to have
An astronomical, monthly
Telephone bill!

The Mailman Comes at 10:00

Our daughter writes dutifully
Every week.
She knows how hungrily
We seek
Each crumb of news
About their days.

They are adapting
To cold weather
And the children
Are finding the delight
Of building snowmen
And riding sleighs.

I miss them so much!
But, Lord,
What a comfort to know
They stay in Your care
Wherever they go.

While We Are Apart

Lord,
This interval without them
Is probably
For the best.

It has brought home
A hard truth
I have secretly
Guessed:

That these young people
Who are so courteous
About us

Are quite capable
Of raising their children
Without us!

The Visit

Guess what, Lord!
As if You didn't know!
I'm going back East
To the ice and snow.
Somehow we've managed
To scrape up the fare,
And Heavens to Betsy!
I'm flying there!

It's incredible, Lord,
How much I've missed them.
So long since I've held them
And hugged them and kissed them.

Oh! Thank You, Lord!
I'm so happy I'm crying,
And ready to forget
I'm scared of flying!

The Homecoming

Lord!
They are coming home!
His company has seen fit
To transfer our
Hard-working son-in-law
Back to the home office.
How thankfully we accept
This latest of Your gifts!

And how anxiously
We await them,
How slowly the clock ticks.
Lord, speed them safely
Along Route 66.

Thanksgiving Grace

The family has gathered again
For the holiday dinner
And we linger at the table,
Well-fed, contented.
Later, the children will be bathed
And put to bed on clean sheets,
Their cheeks pink
With good health.

There are pictures
In the news today
Of hollow-eyed children
Begging in the streets
Of a land far away.

Lord,
Help us to deserve
Such wealth!

Obedience

Lord,
Help me to have the sense
To remain silent
When these children
Are being disciplined.

Their parents
Are wise and intelligent
And have laid down
The rules explicitly.

I must be still,
Even when my heart
Does not agree.

Sibling Love

He wanted a baby brother,
Unable to bear the thought
Of another sister.
When the new arrival
Proved to be a girl,
He threatened to leave home
On the spot!

But he stopped
By the bassinette
On his way,
And that's as far
As he got.

"I Will Not Leave You Comfortless...."

Lord,
I have been thinking today
Of those grandparents
Whose families are in
The missionary field,
Whose loved ones
Are beyond reach and touch,
Whose only contact
Is what torturously slow
And often delayed letters
Can yield.

How hard it must be,
So far away from those children,
Not to hear the young voices,
Not to watch them grow and develop,
Unable to stretch out their arms
And enfold them.

Lord,
In Your mercy,
I am sure you must reserve
A very special kind of comfort
For these grandparents
To uphold them.

Rescue Mission

He has fled to us for refuge,
Disgruntled that his sisters
Are having a slumber party.
He does not want to be
Even in the same county with
All that femininity,
All that giggling
And squealing.

We gladly give him harbor
And make the most of his visit here,
While we can.
We have a feeling
This attitude toward girls
Will barely last
Another year.

My Line of No Resistance

It is my turn to pick up
The littlest one
From nursery school
At noon today.

She skips out
And climbs in the seat
Beside me,
Warm and rumpled,
So innocently sweet...

And within five minutes
Has conned me into
Driving six blocks
Out of my way
To buy her an
Ice-cream treat.

The Miniature

This flaxen-haired child
Is such a replica
Of her mother
She tugs at my heart.

The same level, blue-green eyes,
The same corn-silk braids
With always that tiny wisp
Escaping from the
Center part.

But I must be careful
Not to burden her
With such comparisons of mine,
For she is her own
Little person,
A shining new coin,
Freshly minted
And deserving of
Her own design.

Eternal Season

Lord,
In Your great plan,
Where there is a time
For all things
In due season,
How thankful I am
That there is always a time
For simply enjoying grandchildren,
Those bright-eyed, talkative,
Eager, alert little people,
Inquisitive, curious, questioning,
Cunning and comical,
Ever-changing, never still,
Except when sleeping,
Loving and lovable,
Who give grandparents
Ample reason
For being.

Precious Possession

On her own,
With her birthday money
Folded into the pocket of her jeans,
She heads for the shopping mall...

Past the window filled
With bright, new games,
Past the glittering charms
For her bracelet,
Past another stuffed bear
For her bed,
Past the perfectly darling
Tote bag in red,
Past the siren call,
Unswervingly, of all
The things that little girls
Hold high,
Even, for once,
Past the snowcone stand.

Arrow-straight,
She walks directly
Into the bookstore to buy
Her very own
Young people's Bible,
Phrased in words
She can understand,
So she won't have to use
Her sister's.

Team Effort

Lord,
They have exhausted me today!
"Good sport" Nanny has
Played ball,
Sprinted,
Hopped,
Skipped,
Jumped,
And otherwise gamely
Stayed in the play.

Much as I love them, Lord,
It is with shameless relief
I return them to their mother
And crawl back home
To recuperate
With Ben-Gay.

No Room in the Inn

It is her turn this year
To arrange the manger scene.
She tenderly unwraps the small figures
Whose colors have lost their sheen.

They date back to her own mother's childhood,
And I am too sentimental to replace them.

So this year, Lord,
The tiny stable is crowded.
She insists it is "too cold outside,
They will all freeze!",
And has crammed inside
Everyone and everything,
Including the three wise men,
Joseph and Mary,
Two kneeling camels,
Three cows and a lamb
With a chipped ear,
Six large pine cones
And all the palm trees!

She is a little weak
On horticulture,
But I do not change
What is her own style,
Because at center front
She has placed the Babe,
Still wearing His smile.

The Dinner Party

Come, Lord Jesus,
Be our Guest...

It was a birthday dinner
For me, Lord,
And I sat surrounded
By my smiling family,
With a pile of odd,
Knobby presents
And a birthday cake
With more candles
Than I wanted to count.

The little ones couldn't wait
For me to unwrap the gifts
They had made for me
And Lord,
Amid such love and warmth,
I really don't mind
How the years mount.

And Let These Gifts
To Us Be Blessed.

"I Bring You Good Tidings"

Her mother had labored over
The costume for the Christmas program,
Devising an ingenious contraption
For holding the paper wings in place
And a means of keeping
The halo aloft
With a quivering
Wire brace.

Surely Your angels
Must have smiled!

When she went forward,
On white-stockinged feet,
To recite her part
(Letter perfect),
The halo had slipped,
The wings were askew,
But her message was sweet,
And she melted my heart.

Surely Your angels
Must have smiled!

A Growing Boy

Lord,
You know how very much
We like to have him
Come for a meal...

But he eats with such
Insatiable zeal
That, much as we've always
Loved and adored him,
The day will soon come
When we can't afford him!

The Steward

Lord,
You have given this lad
Such a good, keen mind,
Quick and alert.
Clearly, he is a thinker,
(As well as a whiz at chess!)

Lord,
Help him to keep these talents
Polished and bright,
Active and in good use,
Ready to do Your work
With willingness.

60

The New Roller Skates

For her birthday
She has received
The much longed for
White shoe skates.

She brings them with her
To practice on
Our sidewalk,
And takes an alarming number
Of tumbles and spills,
Always getting up again
With a determined
Smile on her face.

Lord,
I find myself praying
She will always meet
Life's pratfalls
With such grace.

I Have My Limits

They have always had
An assortment of pets,
Cats, dogs, birds,
Even a turtle,
In which I have shown
Dutiful interest,
If not affection.

Tell me, Lord,
Is it absolutely essential
For a grandmother,
Who valiantly tries to be
Loyal and true-blue,
To extend her fondness
To their collection
Of mice, hamsters,
And garter snakes, too?

Picture Lighting

I carry their snapshots
Around in my wallet.
(Grandmotherly pride,
I think we call it.)
They look so refreshingly
Handsome to me,
But Lord, I am more
Than grateful to see,
Beyond the camera,
Yet shining through,
Their pure and simple
Love for You.

Running the Course

She loves to run
And trains vigorously
In after-school trials
For the intercity meet.

We sit in the stands
And watch her race by,
Pale hair streaming,
Taut, young body
Stretched in the stride,
As graceful as a deer,
And as fleet.

She places first,
Breaking the tape
Flushed and teary.

Lord, may she always
Run Your good race
And not weary.

Alfred, the Duck

I keep trying to tell
This good man of mine
That sometimes grandparents
Must accept dubious honors
And childish compliments
With proper respect
(And laughter, too.)

Like having a duck
Named after you!

My Contract Has Not Been Renewed

Lord,
I have been
Scrubbed from the team
And have hung up my jersey,
Too old for the fray,
Wrinkled and gray.

(I can't even begin
To understand
Those video games!)

Lord,
Is this Your gentle way
Of telling me the time
Is now seemly and fitting
For this grandmother
To stick to her knitting?

Delayed Input

Of all the puzzles
And mysteries of life,
It has been the computer
That threw me.

What's worse is having
A twelve-year-old grandson
Explain it
To me!

No Longer the Little One

As the youngest,
She has always
Felt the need to compete,
Stretching her own
Small capacities to meet
Each challenge.

Lord,
It is comforting
To see her now,
So cleareyed and bright,
Her young back so straight and firm,
Finding herself,
Meeting her own goals,
Strengthened by the knowledge,
As she comes into her own,
That she is also
Your own.

Credibility Gap

It comes as a shock to me
That my granddaughters
Simply do not know how
To dry dishes.
They have a proficiency
For loading a dishwasher
And setting the dial.
They consider my linen towel
An antiquity.

I try to tell them
There is a certain, warm
Companionship between women
At this task,
A time for quiet conversation
And homespun intimacy
As dishes are washed
And rinsed.

I do not believe
They are convinced.

Confirmation

Each child, at confirmation,
Has invited us to their own church
To share with them
Their first communion,
The blessed Sacrament
Of bread and wine.

Lord,
Please understand
These tears of mine.

They are tears of
Inexpressible joy
For this precious privilege
Of receiving Your body
And Your blood
Beside these young people.

Thank You, Lord,
For this special blessing.

The Mechanic

Lord,
The years got by me somehow.
I must have been looking
The other way for too long.
Suddenly my grandson
Is a young man
Whom I recognize
Only by his feet
Sticking out from under
His VW.

Lord,
I hesitate to trouble You
With small matters,
But in Your grace,
Could You let us see him
Once in a while
Face to face?

The Collision

She had totaled
Her mother's car
And lay in the hospital,
Unconscious.
We did not know yet
How badly injured.

That is when we used
The Hot Line
In our prayers
To You.

Now she is alert, awake,
With only a headache
And a cut or two
Beneath a small dressing.

Lord, again, again,
Thank You
For this blessing.

No Greater Love

On clear days
He surfaces,
Coming up for air
From the oily depths
Of motor inspection,
From his world
Of carburetors
And radiators.

From what I can see, so far,
Any young lady
Bidding for his attention
Will have to compete
With his car.

Looking Ahead

He has not yet
Chosen a career,
Has not really decided
What he wants to be
Or where he wants to go
With his life.

But he is young,
And for my part
It is sufficient to know
That he has a good head
On his shoulders
And Christ in his heart.

Mother and Daughter Banquet

Once again
The church hall has been
Colorfully decorated
And the long, white tables
Blossom with spring flowers.
My daughter pins a corsage on me,
And the girls flit around
Like butterflies in pretty dressing.
Voices blend into a mounting crescendo
Of laughter and greetings,
Until dinner is called,
And we are silent
For the blessing.

Now there is the hum
Of conversation with good food,
And interlaced through it all,
Weaving up and down each table,
In, out, and around the hall,
Linking generations together,
Woman to child to woman,
Is that long daisy chain of love,
Refreshed each year
In May.

Winds of Tomorrow

Lord,
It bothers me a little
That my granddaughters,
Who know only the
Metallic efficiency
Of automatic dryers,
Will never have
That deep-seated,
Womanly satisfaction
Of pegging laundry on
A clothesline . . .

That feeling of
Summer wind on their arms
As they subdue
Whipping sheets and
Bright towels
That will dry with
The sweet scent of
Clover and sunshine.

But Lord,
I must be forward-looking
And fair.
In Your great wisdom,
No doubt in their
Space-orbiting future,
You will provide
Another such experience
To compare.

Growth Pattern

The trouble with grandchildren
Is that they grow.

They grow *out* of their clothes,
They grow *up* in behavior,
They grow *in* upon themselves,
And sadly, inevitably,
They grow *away*,
Particularly
From grandparents.

Lord,
Can You somehow teach them
That no matter
How distant they seem,
Our love can
Still reach them?

Junior Prom

She shows me the picture
They had taken together,
Formally posed,
She so breathlessly lovely
In her new ball gown
And the rosebud corsage,
The boy so groomed and handsome,
Both smiling and happy.
She tells me his name,
But no more.
She is shy.

Lord,
Why do I suddenly
Want to cry?

The Graduate

The ceremony is held
In the church.
I sit quietly,
Trying to understand
How the years could have
Passed so swiftly.
When his name is called
My heart gives a lurch
And skips a beat.

He is so strong and lean
As he strides up
To receive his diploma,
Nodding a small bow,
Tall in the red cap and gown,
So manly now,
And firm of tread.

Lord,
Go with him
On the road ahead.

Quietly Now

We do not see them as often now, Lord—the grandchildren. They have grown and are so extremely busy with their own affairs and interests. They live their lives at what seems to us to be a frantic pace, but that may be because our own pace has noticeably slowed. We have retired, somewhat thankfully, to the sidelines as loving and caring observers, content with our passive roles now.

We have no idea how we rate as grandparents, but we have always embraced these children in an atmosphere of solid Christian values and steadfast faith. We hope that they will retain warm and fond memories in the years to come, at least enough to repay them for all the pleasure and delight they have given and continue to give us.

In our loving eyes, our grandson is a tall, lean and strikingly handsome young man. His younger sisters are both delicately beautiful. We are proud of each of them, and grateful to their parents for allowing us to be so much a part of their lives. Yes, thank You, Lord, for these grandchildren, for all grandchildren who, unaware, enrich the lives of grandparents.

Dearest Jesus, abide with them!